Witness, I Am

Gregory Scofield

NIGHTWOOD EDITIONS

2016

Nightwood Editions
P.O. Box 1779
Gibsons, BC VON 1V0
Canada
www.nightwoodeditions.com

COVER DESIGN: Angela Yen
COVER IMAGE: "Making Peace With Hurt" by Jeffrey Crowe,
YellowQuill First Nation
TYPOGRAPHY: Carleton Wilson

Canada

Canada Council   Conseil des Arts
for the Arts   du Canada

BRITISH COLUMBIA
ARTS COUNCIL
An agency of the Province of British Columbia

Nightwood Editions acknowledges financial support from
the Government of Canada through the Canada Book Fund and
the Canada Council for the Arts, and from the Province of British Columbia
through the British Columbia Arts Council and the Book Publisher's Tax Credit.

This book has been produced on 100% post-consumer recycled,
ancient-forest-free paper, processed chlorine-free
and printed with vegetable-based dyes.

Printed and bound in Canada.

CIP data available from Library and Archives Canada.

ISBN 978-0-88971-323-9

Contents

Muskrat Woman

for nimâmâsis, Georgina

Muskrat Woman

This poem is a retelling, a reimagining of a much longer âtayôhkêwina—Cree Sacred Story. In my teachings, one is not supposed to say kistêsinâw's (elder brother's) other name, "wîsahkêcâhk," during the summer months. It is considered inappropriate to use his name when there is no snow on the ground.

I

miyaskâm kinwês   *After a long time*

He says, *Get me a piece*
Of the old earth.
She says, *Fuck you!*
Get your own dirt.

He says, *awâs! Get me*
Some of the old earth.   *Go away*
Fuck you! She says.
Get your own dirt.

He says, *Get me a piece*
Of the old earth
Or I'll smash you.
She says, *hâw, acimo!*
Tell the story.

But in the garden
With the blooming tree
She thinks to herself,
I have no right
To be melancholy.
My life is exquisite.

Now her eyes
Are two black beads,
The kind of bad luck

9

On her rosary.
hâw, acimo! she says.
Not before the old earth, he says.

Tell the story

Then her paws slip
Into the consonants
Of her old name,
The sound of mud.

It was true.
She was a dreary old cynic.
But she had those rights.
She left good cheer the day
The Black Robe stunk
On top of her. In his hunger
He called out the other names,
The ones like Ramona,
Alberta, Delphine, Roxanne
And Lana. Those names
He left on a highway.

But mostly with her
He cried, *Oblige me.*
The wafer of his tongue
Was his weapon and so, too,
Were his hymns and prayers.
He made her believe
In the implication of loneliness.
The bricks of that place
Eventually made her eyes go dim.
It made her hate the old earth.
So she had rights.

A short time after
His careful thinking,
He says, *Get me a piece
Of the old earth.*

Fuck you, she says.
Get your own dirt.

His hand was quick,
So much so her mouth
Exploded like a parasol,
The bones of her face
Stretching tight, tight her skin.

He says, *Get me some*
Of the old earth. sîmak!   *Right away*
Fuck you, she says.
Get your own dirt.

His hand was quick.
This time her two front teeth,
The cutting ones went loose
Like snare wire, the den
Of her mouth empty.

Tell the story, she says.
Fuck you, he says.
Tell your own story.

kisêyiniw said it was   *Old Man*
Her own damn fault.
He grumbled about
Her being a dumb bitch
And gave everyone
The burden of suffering.

Some say that is what
Made her hitchhike
On the highway.
But her borrowed rib
Just rotted away,
All worm-kissed

11

Like the fruit she gave him,
The one who cried
And promised to tell
The story. He even sang
His grandfather's song,
The lullaby for Water Beings.

The highway was her last resort.
She simply wanted air.
But in the bush that night,
Clinging to her breath,
She dreamt she dove into
The water, an endless silk ribbon
Taking her down and down
To where she could see everything.
It was so clear, the Old World.
Her sisters had their own ribs.
They were growing fruit trees,
So many they had little use
For collective guilt.

By the sweetest tree
Her nôhkom met her.   *grandmother*
She said, *My girl,*

Once you were wacaskw   *muskrat*
But your real name
Is Swimming-with-a-bundle.
Back then you liked to collect
All sorts of things. One time
You took a male, a female
Of each animal. You made a boat
With your teeth, the cutting ones.
You made a boat with two birch trees
And with pitch you made it float.

She thought about what her granny said.

Above her came the sweet sound of singing.
She was certain she heard two voices.
Then she said to her nôhkom,

Yes, it's odd no one thought
To call me wise. But there again
I am brown and my names
Hadn't been spit into existence,
The ones like squaw and cunt.
Those came on a different boat.
Those landed with a new tongue.
I tried to drown them
But they wouldn't sink.
So I put them in my bundle
And starved them of light.

Then she said, sucking on
The fruit her granny gave her:

And then there were the names
I collected before the investigation.
Those ones I took from the farm.
I dug up with a backhoe.
They had to be sifted like flour.
There were bones, too,
Without names. Those ones
I wrapped in red cloth
Before I put them in my bundle.
I called them wacaskw   *muskrat*
After myself because
Jane Doe had no sound.

Then it started piss-pouring rain.
So I crammed all those animals
Onto my boat. When we were away
From him, I started singing
The names. I sang them like this:

13

Mona, hey-ya-hey-yow
Marnie, hey-ya-hey-yow
Andrea, hey-ya-hey-yow
Sereena, hey-ya-hey-yow
Georgina, hey-ya-hey-yow
Brenda, hey-ya-hey-yow

The others I sang, too.

She was brown
And all those names
Lived in her pulse.

But then his song
Pulled her to the surface:

Get me a piece of the old earth,
He says, And I'll make plenty
Of roots for you to eat.
I will create rushes so you
Can make a nice house.

wâcistakâc! she says.   Oh, my goodness.
What kind of house?

Now her eyes are two skipping stones,
The kind born to young women.

It'll have a big kitchen, he says.
So many pots and pans,
You'll never tire of cooking.

ekwa nânitaw
kahkiyâw nîcisânak?   And what about my sisters?

Hmm, he says.
It's only accessible

14

By bush plane or boat.

Then he shows his pretty teeth.
He didn't want to speak about boats.

Fuck you! she says. *Get your own dirt.*

kisêyiniw had a hard time   *Old Man*
Controlling her. She was all tedious
Like twisted string. Too many knots
And not enough rope to hold her down.
With her umbilical cord she passed
Those aggravations down
And by Jesus, it took a patient man
To unravel his son's sensibilities.
They say she was once a good old boy.
Therefore it only took minor coaxing,
A dare, a promise of pussy.
Pussy was a name he took from the bag
Of his scrotum. He performed it for his boys.
He liked the way it rolled off his tongue.

Still she made no excuses.
She drafted the blueprints
And went about designing her boat,
In secret. Not that she was ashamed.
But even her sons
Couldn't be trusted.
Only her nôhkom knew.   *grandmother*
There was the issue
Of safe places, not for the animals
But for the names.
otîcisâna owîhowiniyiwa.   *Her sisters' names*
After quibbling over semantics
She decided it best to make
1,200 rooms with the ability
To add on. The animals, the names

15

She'd float until the water receded.
And she didn't give a good goddamn
Whether it rained or not.

II

ispihk kahkiyâw kîkway
ka-kî-mâcipayin   *In the beginning*

After kise-manito   *The Creator*
Made all the animals,
The first people,
He said to niskam-nâpêw,   *First Man*
Who depending on the day,
Also answered
To wîsahkêcâhk or Adam:

Take good care of my people,
And teach them how to live. Show them
The plants and roots that will kill them
Teach them to respect my creation.
Do not let the animals, the people quarrel.

But he didn't listen. He let creatures
Do as they wished and soon there was
Much quarrelling and shedding of blood.

If you do not keep
The ground clean,
Said kisêyiniw, *I will take*   *Old Man*
Everything from you.

But he did not believe the Creator.
He became more and more careless
And disobedient. He tricked the animals
And people, and soon the earth
Was red with blood.

niskam-iskwew,   *First Woman*
who depending on kisêyiniw's mood,

17

Employed gentle reasoning.
At first she said:

Such is a lovely green, our Paradise,
The kaleidoscopic flowers
Bending to us their lazy heads.
Bow down, bow down, my love
The earth is but their stage.

But he was not moved.
Not in the least.

Then she thought it best
To reason with fact.

I smell rain! she said.

But still he did not listen.

This time kisêyiniw   *Old Man*
Became very angry.

I will take everything from you
And wash the ground clean, he said.

Still Adam did not believe the Creator.
He was reclining in the orchard,
Watching the outcome
Of two serpents fighting.
His money was on
The barrel-chested one,
The one the announcer called
Original Sin. The other one
Was introduced as *Fall of Man*
Although wîsahkêcâhk,
Now eating his dripping plum,
Yelled out, *Crybaby, crybaby!*

Then it started to rain.

êkwa ka-kimiwahk   *And it rained*

ka-kimiwahk   *It rained*

Day after day, night after night
The rains continued.
The water in the lakes and rivers
Rose higher and higher.
At last they overflowed their banks
And washed the ground clean.

niskam-iskwew was   *First Woman*
Nowhere to be found.

But in his head that was held up
By his backbone that was connected
To his neck bone which was connected
To his breastbone in which lived his heart,
The complicated thing, he heard:

Such is a lovely green, our Paradise,
The kaleidoscopic flowers
Bending to us their lazy heads.
Bow down, bow down, my love
The earth is but their stage.

The sea came up on the land.
All was lost except
Otter, Beaver and Muskrat.
niskam-nâpêw tried   *First Man*
To stop the sea
But it was too strong.
Then Adam sat on the water
And wept. Otter, Beaver
And Muskrat sat beside him,

19

Resting their heads
On one of his thighs.

In time the rain stopped
But the sea covered the land.
wîsahkêcâhk took courage
But he did not dare speak
To the Creator.
After long and sad thoughts
About his misery,
niskam-nâpêw said   *First Man*
To himself:

If I could get a bit of the old earth
Beneath the water, I could make
An island for us to live on.

wîsahkêcâhk did not have the power
To create anything
But he did have the ability
To expand what was already created.
Because he could not dive
And because he did not know
How far it was to the old earth,
He did not know what to do.

Taking pity on him,
kise-manito said,   *The Creator*

I will give you the power
To remake everything
If you use the old materials
Buried under the water.

Adam thought this was quite fine.
In fact he was relieved
All he had to do was float

Alongside Otter, Beaver and Muskrat
Although one night
When the moon was full,
Singing like a schoolgirl,
He was certain he heard
The sound of his own rib laughing.

Floating on the flood,
He said to the three animals beside him:

We shall starve unless one of you
Can bring me a bit of the old earth.
If you get it for me
I'll make an island for us to live.

He turned to Otter:

You are brave and strong.
If you dive into the water
And bring me some old earth
I'll make plenty of fish for you to eat.

Beaver thought
This was reasonable.
Otter agreed.
But niskam-nâpêw   *First Man*
Could do better,
Muskrat thought.
For example he could make
A body of bones,
The bundle belonging
To that young woman.
She was twenty, that girl.
She was twenty and left
In a farmer's field.
wîsahkêcâhk could do better,
Muskrat thought.

21

He could make the licence plate,
Show the face of the man
Who took her. Adam could
Do better, Muskrat thought.
He could request a national call-out,
A media blitz. After all, her voice lived
In sixty-one seconds of audio,
Frozen on her cell phone.

Where are we by?

We're just headin' south of Beaumont,
Or north of Beaumont.

We're headin' north of Beaumont.
No, where are we going?

The back roads.

Are you fucking kidding me?

No, I'm not kidding you.

You better not be taking me
Anywhere I don't want to go.
I want to go to the city, okay?
No, we're not going in the city are we?

Yes we are, we're going...

No we're not. Then where the fuck
Are these roads going to?

To Fiftieth Street.

Fiftieth Street? Are you sure?

Absolutely.

Yo, where are we going?

Fiftieth Street.

Fiftieth Street? East, right?

East.

He could do so much better,
Muskrat thought.
But then Otter dived.
He came up without
Reaching the ground.

kîhtwâm! wîsahkêcâhk said.   *Again*

So Otter dived again.
He came up without
Reaching the ground.

Thou shalt not despair, Adam said.
Labour is our duty,
Which we must faithfully perform.
It is part of man's sentence,
Which idleness daringly defies.

A third time Otter went below
The surface. nama kîkway.   *Nothing*
When he returned,
He was so weary
He could not dive again.

You're a coward!
niskam-nâpêw said.   *First Man*
I know Beaver can dive

23

To the bottom of the flood.
He'll put you to shame.

Then he turned to Beaver:

You are brave and wise.
If you dive into the water
And bring me a bit of the old earth,
I will make a good house
For you on a new island.
You will be warm in the winter.
Now dive straight down,
As a brave beaver does.

Otter thought this was
Overly generous.
niskam-nâpêw could do better,   *First Man*
Muskrat thought.
He could, if he wanted,
Make an island as desolate
As mud. There he could put
The perpetrators of silence,
Let them ring their holy bells.
He could, if he wanted,
Make them eat wîhtikow soup,   *cannibal*
Let them choke on
The names they've taken.

And so beaver dived. Twice.
And twice he returned
Without any earth.

Dive once more, niskam-nâpêw said.
If you bring me a bit of the old earth,
I'll make you a wife.

24

Once again Beaver went below
The surface. So niskam-nâpêw could
Make a woman, Muskrat thought.
He was upping the stakes,
Willing to forfeit a rib.

Beaver stayed so long
Everyone feared him dead.
Finally he came back
Almost lifeless, no earth
In his paws.

Goddamn it! Adam said.

wîsahkêcâhk was very sad.
If Otter and Beaver
Couldn't reach the old earth,
Surely Muskrat would fail.

Otter and Beaver are fools,
niskam-nâpêw said to Muskrat.
They got lost.
If you dive into the water
And bring me a bit of the old earth,
I will make plenty of roots
For you to eat.
I will create rushes
So you can make
A nice house
With rushes and dirt.

Surely, Muskrat thought,
If niskam-nâpêw
Could make such a fine house,
He could make a big kitchen
With plenty of pots and pans.
A table, too, with a fancy oil cloth,

25

Every flower of Paradise
Blooming across its surface.
Muskrat wanted bone-china cups,
Too. Not the chipped kind
From Sally Ann, but the good ones
From England, maybe even
The ones slobbered on by the Queen.

And Muskrat wanted
To be called Queen.
She wanted her own kind
Of talk. kayâs-askiy.   *Old earth*
Not this Original Sin talk
Or the thumping of chests.
She wanted some sister time.
e-nîcisânak.   *Her sisters*
Plain and simple.

Sister time. That was it.
That's all she wanted.

III

ê-oskaskipayik   *When the world becomes new*

She thought, her brain
Not yet waterlogged,
She will bite a list
Onto birch bark.
A list made by her teeth
And spit. This list, Muskrat thought,
Will be as long as it is
To the Old World.
With each metre down,
She knew, there will be
Names. a-hâ mihcêtowîhkât   *Yes, many names*

Once niskam-iskwew   *First Woman*
Heard a rumour.
The ocean is divided
Into three zones
Based on depth and light level.
Although some creatures
Depend on light to live,
Adam had said,
Others can do without it.
niskam-nâpêw, she was certain,   *First Man*
Meant those iskwêwak like: *women*

Pine Leaf, the Crow war leader,
Who like her fellow male chiefs,
Also took several wives.

Muskrat sniffed the water.

And then there was Lozen,
Who fought in numerous battles

27

Alongside Geronimo
In the last campaign
Of the Apache Wars.

The water is like
My câpân's looking glass,   *great-grandmother's*
She thought.

And Buffalo Calf Road Woman,
Who charged into the centre
Of battle to save her brother
Whose horse had been shot
Out from under him.

She touched the water,
Thinking about
Her nôhkom's beadwork.   *grandmother*

And then there was Moving Robe,
She counted, who during the Battle
Of the Greasy Grass in Montana,
Led a counterattack against
The US Calvary. So formidable her,
Muskrat thought.

She extended a foot like a ballerina.
Ho! she squealed, *the water*
Is warm today.
Ah! she said *it's as warm*
As my mother's womb.

And then she counted
All of the others.
The ones from history.
The ones from battles.
The ones forgotten.

And the ones who depended
On the light. And the ones
Left in the dark.

This she did out loud
So the names were pulled
From the depths.
So they were given light,
All of these iskwêw names.   *woman*

You will find the ground
If you dive straight down,
wîsahkêcâhk said at last.

And so Muskrat dove head-first
Into the water. Down and down
And down she went, loosening
More names like barnacles.
Then up to the surface she came
Wearing a dress of names.

Jesus Christ! Adam muttered
Under his breath.

Now, now nicîmos,   *Sweetheart*
niskam-nâpêw coaxed,   *First Man*
I will keep safe your beautiful dress,
But you must get me
A piece of the old earth.

This time kise-manito   *The Creator*
Said to wîsahkêcâhk:

If you do not keep this dress
Clean and safe
I will make you blind.

And so Muskrat dived a second time.
So long was she gone
That her dress began speaking:

I *am sacred,* said one sleeve.
I *am holy,* said the other.
I *am blessed,* said the collar.

I *am hallowed,* said the buttonhole.
I *am consecrated,* said the hemline.
I *am holy,* said the bodice.
I *am sacred,* said the breast.
I *am to be loved,* said the other.

When she returned,
Wearing a swallowtail of new names,
All stitched like falling stars,
niskam-nâpêw, twisting in his bones,
Let go of his voice:

Goddamn it, Jesus Christ
And all of the saints!

Now, now nicîmos, Adam coaxed,   *Sweetheart*
Let me see your beautiful fingers,
*Your exquisite toes.*This time kise-manito said
To wîsahkêcâhk:

If you harm this swallowtail,
I will make you mute.

And so she extended her right paw.

I *smell the smell of earth,* wîsahkêcâhk sang.

Then the names began to assemble.
They moved into a circle,

Their eyes wide open.
One name, an oceanographer
She'd aspired to be,
Stepped inside of the circle.

Sisters, she began.
My knowledge is my bundle
Humble as it may be.
I own nothing, êy-êy!   exclamation of humility
Except for the letters of my name.
I own nothing, êy-êy!
Except for the sound of it spoken.
I own nothing, êy-êy!
Except for this small bundle
Of knowledge I am now going
To tell. I am going to tell
This knowing to you, sisters.
êy-êy!

And so she unwrapped
Her bundle and the sister names
Received her teaching.

The ocean, she told them, *is this deep.*

40 metres will be
Maximum depth for scuba divers.

301 metres will be
Height of the Eiffel Tower.

500 metres will be
The deepest blue whales can dive.

1,000 metres will be
The maximum depth sunlight reaches.

1,828 metres will be
The lowest point of the Grand Canyon.

4,267 metres will be
The average depth of the ocean.

8,850 metres will be
The height of Mount Everest.

10,898 metres will be the depth
Director James Cameron reaches in 2012.

10,994 metres will be the depth
Don Watson and Jacques Piccard reach in 1960.

11,034 metres will be the
Bottom of the Mariana Trench.

She carefully tied up her knowledge,
The oceanographer.
This, she concluded,
Is where Muskrat will find
The old earth. ekosi! êy-êy!   *I am done*

For the first time niskam-iskwew
Felt she owned her own rib.
She didn't need to keep apologizing
For the breath he gifted her.
Then she spoke to the names she'd collected.

I wish to be called Mariana,
She said. *But my name*
Is wacaskw-iskwêw.   *Muskrat Woman*

And so she extended her left paw.

I smell the smell of earth, sang Adam.

Go again, niskam-nâpêw said.
If you bring me even a small piece of earth
I will make a husband for you.

A husband? Mariana asked. *Will he trap me?*

No, wîsahkêcâhk said.
He will be gentle with words.

Will he skin me? she asked.

No, Adam said.
I will make him soft of hands.

Will he eat me? She asked.

niskam-nâpêw thought
About the old ground and how
He'd eaten freely of all the trees
In the garden, except for the one tree
He was prohibited from eating.

No, wîsahkêcâhk finally said.
I will make him content.

Then the names began to assemble.
They moved into a circle,
Their eyes wide open.
Another name, an old woman
She'd aspired to be,
Stepped inside the circle.

Sister, she told Muskrat,
You will bear a great many children.
Have a strong heart now.
Go straight down,
As far as you can go.

33

êkwa! She clapped,
kôhkîpayiho! kôhkîpayiho!   *Now dive quickly!*

This time Mariana stayed so long
Otter and Beaver, wîsahkêcâhk
Feared she had drowned.
At last they saw some bubbles
Coming up through the water.
wîsahkêcâhk reached his long arm down,
Seized Muskrat and pulled her up
Beside them. She was almost dead,
But against her breast in her forepaws
She held a piece of the old earth –

kayâs askîy.   *Old earth*

kayâs askîy.

kayâs askîy.

Joyously, wîsahkêcâhk seized the earth,
And in a short time
He expanded it into an island.

This time kise-manito   *The Creator*
Said to wîsahkêcâhk.

If you do not keep the ground clean,
I will take everything from you.
In this dream
Far from the highway,
Far from the farm,
She floated in her boat,
Fishing for the names
To keep safe in her bundle.

These she caught by singing,

By keening to a water bird.

She sang for the pêpisisak first –   *babies*

Tamara, hey-ya-hey-yow
Natasha, hey-ya-hey-yow

The other babies she sang, too.
Their names she caught by singing,
By keening to a loon.

Then she sang for
The oskinîkiskwêwak –   *young women*

Tina, hey-ya-hey-yow
Felicia, hey-ya-hey-yow
Helen, hey-ya-hey-yow
Theresa, hey-ya-hey-yow
Amber, hey-ya-hey yow

The other young women
She sang for too. Their names
She caught by singing,
By keening to a swan.

Then she sang for
The iskwêwak –   *women*

Bella, hey-ya-hey-yow
Margaret, hey-ya-hey-yow
Belinda, hey-ya-hey-yow
Tanya, hey-ya-hey-yow
Krystal, hey-ya-hey-yow

The other women she sang for too.
Their names she caught by singing,
By keening to a crane.

Then she sang
For the nôtokêwak –   *old women*

Mary, hey-ya-hey-yow
Cora, hey-ya-hey-yow

The other old women she sang for too.
Their names she caught by singing,
By keening to a magpie.

ê-oskaskipayik   *When the world becomes new*
She pondered.

After wîssahkêcâhk
Obtains some wood
From which he'll make trees.

After niskam-nâpêw   *First Man*
Obtains some bones
From which he'll make
The second race of animals.

After it is told, kise-manito   *The Creator*
Will remake all things.

After Adam commands the rivers
To take the salt water back to the sea.

After Otter and Beaver,
Kisêyiniw announce   *Old Man*
Themselves cured.

After they leave office.

After the DNA of thirty-three women
Is found on the farm.

36

After it is ruled their bones
Are worth second-degree.

After all of the names come home.

After she has a dry place
On which to lay her bundle.

miyasâm kinewês   *After a long time*
She thought.

But this world after,
She remembered,
Is a long time.

All of these things
She'd float in her boat

Until the water receded.
And she didn't give
A good goddamn
Whether it rained or not.

Get me a piece of the old earth,
He says. *Fuck you!* she says.
Get your own dirt.

Ghost Dance

for niwâhkômâkanak, those who travelled beyond

Magnificent Liar

lay down with me, give me your lips
fall onto me your words of praise,
your famished tongue a celebration

give to me, in this terrible hour
the hope I am worth
the tinker of your hands

lay down with me
lay down with me, remake me
in this useless hour

give to me your unbound limbs
fall onto me your applause
bravo, bravo

give to me the prospect of this,
your tongue, your lips
the hope I am worth such jubilee

lay down with me, let loose the day
this miserable hour
fall onto me your words of praise

fall onto me your hands
let me be certain of their credibility
fall onto me your tongue,

your perfectly steered tongue
your lips, your lips
so captive in their singing.

Prayer for the Man Who Raped Her

I could pray you are visited by the cannibal
Tonight in the last rays of light
Wherever you are, you might be lying quiet
Forgetful in your bones
You might be smoking, sucking deep your breath
You could be watching the last of the day
That sliver of hope
Illuminating the beads on the vest she made you

I pray your mother good rest
I pray your sister the peace of stars
I pray your grandmother easy breath

I could pray you are visited by the cannibal
In our language
She called them wîhtikow, the dead ones
Whose taste for flesh made them unholy
Forgetful in their bones
Although in my dreaming they lived in the bush
The darkness, places beyond the street lamps
The little house with an open front door
Her kitchen table

I pray your mother the peace of stars
I pray your sister easy breath
I pray your grandmother good rest

I could pray you are visited by the wîhtikow
Where I am it is evening and
Tonight two loons will call on the lake
I am here in my bed
Unpacking the stories she told me
Once there was an old man, he was hungry for flesh
Forgetful in his bones
They killed him with ice to his heart

I pray your mother easy breath
I pray your sister good rest
I pray your grandmother the peace of stars

Killer

It could happen in June.
The first day of begonias.
In a suburb as quiet as a bullet.

I could kill you far beyond
the confines of the law.
I could take your fingers,
snap them one by one,

this one for the funny man,
this one for chef,
this one for the gardener,
this one for the monk,
that one for the archivist.

I could take both of your hands,
heavy as they are, drag them
to a ravine as deep as my back.
I could chew them to nubs,
the warm fleshy things.

I could kill you without fuss.
I could kiss you to death,
this tongue for the nipple,
these teeth for your throat.

I could hide the evidence,
toss it in a bag.
Wrap you in a sheet.
Drown you in the shower.

I could kill you far beyond
the neighbour's eye. I could
take what's left of your body,
scour clean my tracks.

I could, this first day
of sweetening blooms,
take your fingers,
tie them down one by one.

This one for the runaway,
this one for the joker,
this one for the sass-talker,
this one for the judge,
that one for the jury.

Oh, I could kill you.

Hospital Dream

In this dream
there is a body of water between us.
Somewhere you lay in a room
making sounds from spittle.
Somewhere is the sound of sanity
refracting in pools of light,
the fish of your words
held by the line of the nurse beside you.

I'm here to collect what's left of your bones.
But he is here also, the collector
to break what's left of the good ones.
I cannot make a net to catch you.
I can only swim to witness your unravelling,
a child without clothes on.
Why do you allow him the chair
at the foot of your bed? I cannot see

the mirror you see, the goodness.
Mother, you are such a mess of limbs.
Everything is spilling out, your heart and hope.
I'm given the task to collect these things.
And he is here with his hook, fishing.
In this dream there is a body of water
between us. And I cannot swim
fast enough to save you.

Convalescence

Don't pity me.
These are scars from war.
Today they are red like ribbons.
Tomorrow they might be gone.

In an office without windows
the young doctor says,
There! There! We'll get you all sorted out.
I'm his practice, his module from medical school.

The terrible breathing has been two months in.
A fighting dog lives in my chest, snarling.
At night it is ugly when the air is thin.
My poor man, all unarmed to this, is two golden hands.

There! There! he says. *We'll get you all sorted out.*
And always in the morning my feet are pointed onward.
Again they are set right to carry my mother,
who, falling in her skin, I held up like a bridge pier.

There! There! I said. *We'll get you all sorted out.*
Still the ribbons flutter on the crest of a bluff.
Today they are red.
Tomorrow they might be gone.

Apparently it will be between two and four weeks
for the miracle to begin working.
The orange pill is the bridge.
It is to keep one from utter collapse.

In the meantime the snow is leaving.
Day by day I dream myself away from the witnessing,
the matted roots of all I cannot un-see.
There! There! I say. *We'll get you all sorted out.*

Sending You Away on a Boat of Your Making

Do not ask me to excuse you.
I'm sending you away
on this boat of your making.

   Here are my shoulders,
   the sail of your silence.
   Here is my spine,
   the rudder of your negligence.

Do not ask me to pity you.
Here I am almost ancient, suspicious,
carefully moored to all docks of leaving.

   This is my breath,
   the funnel of your apathy.
   These are my feet, cautious and bare,
   the gangplank of your building.

I am sending you away
on this boat of your making.
Do not ask me to praise you.

   Here are my eyes, stormy blue.
   Here are my eyes, two grey pelicans.
   Here are my eyes, black as the gunwale.
   Here are my eyes, the propeller.

Do not anchor yourself here.
Do not ask me to welcome you.
Do not say I am your cargo.

These are my ribs,
the port of your departure.
In her you set sail,
away from my ghetto.

These are my ribs,
the stateroom in which I keep you as stowage.
Do not ask me to give you light.

Ghost Dance

then

I will paint my shirt
with earth and sky,
crows and magpies

when the sun goes into shadow
I will lay myself down
and in my breath
I will see the heavens, I will see

you

and I will dance, I will dance
my face dappled in stars
and on my neck
will hang your lips, owl feathers

swift, swift
in their flight calling me
to fall down, to humble my bones
in the lilt of your singing,

then

you will paint me in red ochre
my shirt, this skin
no longer torn and tattered
and I will rise,

I will dance this passage of time,
I will dance the moon,
I will dance the bullets of fear,
I will dance the bullets of sorrow,

I will take flight, a sky bird
drawn in pigments of blue and yellow,
then I will be new,
holy in the light of your face.

Poem for the Group of Seven

In soft Cree minor

Each day there is news
Some say the scout is circling
By the lake, above the clouds
He is sweeping clean the sky

    nîsta, I cannot see the lake   *Myself*
    The lake is not what I can see

They say he is carrying the sun
They say he is looking to make camp
âh, maskihkîwan, maskihkîwan   *There are medicines present*
They say he is coming home

    I am not home, nîsta   *Myself*
    Here I am not home

Each day there is news
Soon they say
His relatives will come
pê-kiwê, pê-kiwê   *Come home, come home*

Soon they say
The trees will be singing
âh, nihtâ-nikamo, nihtâ-nikamo   *It will be beautiful singing*
They say he will give them back their voice

He will give them back their songs
Luminous in their budding
This he will do
awas kîwêtin, kisinôhtin   *Be gone northern wind, cold wind*

nîsta, my voice is not here
    My voice is not here

Each day there is news
The grey heads of stones
He is about to make them blush
miyo-âcimo, âh, miyo-âcimo   *He tells a good story*

He is circling
The scout by the lake

Poet

They did not say
he would see this aperture.
They did not say
the light would be temporary, the rays

of which he is left to winnow.
They did not say
he would be fixed in space,
hanging from his own apparatus.

They did not say
he would see this age.
They did not say
he would be held in static, swinging

from his own words, floating the lines
into stanzas
he believed would change the world.
They did not say

he would be anything but aerial.
In fact, they did not say
his rope would be painted in watercolour.
Oh, this they did not say.

He arrived on the tail swing of Ginsberg and Kerouac.
He arrived too late for nights of fucking,
for groupies who swelled in their beds at night,
reading him like God.

Now he stumbles on the death fall
of Sexton and Plath and
they will not give him the zenith
back to the stars, back to the bitch coyote

who bore him, the poet.

Cripple

I say things like,

Ruminator! Nutjob!
You're the problem of everything.

But still he sips from the thin cup of hope.
These are the sounds his body makes,
heave ho, heave ho!
At least is the theory.

I do my best to chase him away.
I give him my best scowl.

His tongue is as useless
as a board of bent nails.
Other times it's as quick as a mouse,

rushing through the doorway of doubt.
The poor thing is saucer-eyed,
the last of its courage
spilling onto the pavement of hope.

Some say it's apropos to the condition,
the mad scramble toward reasoning.
Still I do my best to chase him away.
I muster up things like,

Bravo! Bravo! He writes a poem.
Now go, go!

Some days, given the decibel of silence,
I am prone to ugliness.
I hurl my clichés. I spit things like,

Take your desperation and shove it!
Take your fear and embrace it.

But always, no matter the morning,
I give him the pill.

The tiny blue one to regulate his pulse.
At night the white one
that nails him to the bed.

Mostly in the mornings
as he stumbles into day,
I am resonant of his breaks.
I am vigilant of his limbs.

I say things like,

This is good. You are good.
You are moving. Your legs are strong.
Jubilant is the stride of your feet.

Now walk, dear boy. Walk!
Here is the kitchen. Here is the cupboard.
It holds everything.

Dangerous Love

This could be about making soup   how

I take the chicken, hacked to the bone,

Run it under cold water

Dissolving any blood left by the butcher   how

I carefully place this disarticulation

Into lukewarm water

As if I am bathing a baby, as if

I believe this baptism cleansing   how

I take the onion, tucked in its skin,

Slice the poor bastard in two

Coaxing only its flavour, its ability to golden

The broth I am making

This liquid of love   how

I take two carrots, two stalks of celery

Behead and push them down between the hopeless thighs

Heartbreaking in the last of their pinkness   how

I march to the garden, the pious planter, the patient tender

Set my hand upon the rosemary, the thyme, the sage

The green heads of parsley

Snap their delicate bones

Me, the terrorist, the death-row conductor   how

I sing for the gas, the licking flame   how

I add to this stewing wound salt, pepper, a dash of powdered stock,

The thought of a clawed foot

Stirred by my grandmother's hand   how

These collected things are not mine

But owning to the house, the rooms

Where we make love and war, where we get lost

In conversations that go way too late   how

We sip the golden miracle

Long after our bodies take comfort

Panic

Mostly it comes on the thin breath of night,
The ending song of the day
Silk in its slinking, quickly
It moves. Quickly it pitches.

It could be joyous depending on the day.
It could be all splinters the next.
Either way, it loves me.
I am its score. It conducts me.

I am its chest with twelve beating drums.
I am its nostrils with two wobbly notes.
I am its trumpet sounding my bones.
I am the empty chair of the flutist.

Once it pinned me to the bed and
Kept me there for three days.
I was all nerves and too many eyes.
My feet thought they were going away.

In the terrible symphony
I saw my lungs turn into powder.
I saw my tongue roll over on itself.
Then the orchestra nearly packed up.

It had two horns and a pointed chin.
The very image of my mother's making
In her time away, her fractured head
Reorganized into some newly zapped package.

It kissed my lips and from my strappings,
I rose like Icarus. I said, *Enough*
Before I bit its poisonous tongue.
Then the true conductor came and I began to play.

Still it comes on the thin breath of night,
All its golden gadgets set to sounding.
It is true. It loves me.
I am its brimming ovation.

This Is How the Heart Breaks
for Dixie

Scrubbing what can't be seen.
The countertop in laughing light.

It comes to this. All year
the demolition of the house.

First it is the living room
where she is apt to lay. Then the hall

because it's a tunnel, a passage
as long as hope.

And then the bedroom and on the duvet,
two heavy eyes, a pauper's flame at best.

We are suffering this unmaking,
this teardown of something so precious.

I am beyond my own bed of grief.
It happens like this. Fall into winter,

the stripping of the rooms.
The rapid theft. The rupture of pipes.

The pilfering of anything recognizable.
God will not give a miracle.

He is boarding her windows.
Tap, tap, tap.

It comes to this. Spring
I'm living in the ghost of her bones.

I lift her from the hallway,
offer her face to the light. It comes to this,

the moment of fracture. The brimming of rage.
And then the invocation,

laying down my petition.
There will be no miracle.

There is only the thinning leaves of August
and how to pack her tiny toes.

It comes to this. My love, dimming the lights,
lifting her to a faraway home.

Almost Gone

My mother languished in that place three whole years. Weekly they
marked the parts of her they said were broken. They believed, as do the
faithful, Cerletti's invention could cure her. They believed they could
save her from walking in the woods, away from the city and the black
before the first sun rises. Instead they took her words, the cool lip of
the lake and the tongue of the trees, in particular, the paper birch in
mid-summer when the leaves all aflutter and musical in their thinking
pirouette their silk heels before bowing.

And each week they arrived like soldiers, perfect in their shoes, glorious
in their group. They held the form under her chin like a bowl, chanting
I should be given hope, her small appendage. But the northern part
of her, the geese when they fly home kept precise her direction. My
mother languished in that place three whole years. There they stole her
language, the words to paint us home. Still, in her long dreaming, she
never forgot to say, *No*.

Dangerous Sound

for niwicewâkan, Mark

Untitled

I was born into this fair skin
A long way from a fair land
A long way from home

I was born with my right foot crooked
A long way from the mountaintop
A long way from home

Into this fair skin I came
môniyâw, môniyâw   *white person*
A long way from home

My right foot crooked
I was born at the bottom of the mountain
A long way from home

Fair in my skin, fair in this housing
I was born to be unseen
môniyâw, môniyâw

A long way from home
In this fair land
I was born

I was born at the bottom of the mountain
I was born into this fair skin
A long way from home

In this fair skin I was born to be unseen
nanâskom, nanâskom the red ochre   *I am grateful*
I come from on the mountain

Scraps

I was born to eat at everyone else's table
Here a scrap, there a scrap
I am just a scrap, scrap

I was born to the sound of my mother's footsteps
Echoing gone, gone
Long gone

I was born to the sound of her love
Aching in this room
Called my memory

I was born to sit at everyone else's table
Here a crumb, there a crumb
I am just a crumb, crumb

I can say,   I   can   say
I have been fed by Whites
I have been fed by Indians
I have been fed by Breeds
I have been fed by Jews
I have been fed by Straights
I have been fed by Gays

I am good at sucking the bones they throw me
Here a bone, there a bone
I am just a bone, bone

I was born to the stillness of my father's heartbeat
Thu-thu-umping
Away from my own unintelligible beat

I can say,   I   can   say
I have been starved by Whites
I have been starved by Indians

I have been starved by Breeds
I have been starved by Jews
I have been starved by Straights
I have been starved by Gays

I am good at sucking the marrow
From my own bones
In times of uncertainty

I was born to eat at everyone else's table
Here a scrap, there a scrap
I am just a scrap, scrap

I was born to sit at everyone else's table
Here a crumb, there a crumb
I am just a crumb, crumb

I was born in a time of plenty
I was born in a time of prosperity
I was born with my two feet

Dangling, my mouth hungry
The words like a feast
Fattening the souls of everyone else

But here I sit
A stranger at my own table

Here I sit in a time of plenty
Here I sit in a time of prosperity

Here I sit with my two feet dangling
My mouth hungry

The words like a feast
Fattening the souls of everyone else

This Is an Honour Song for Billy Jack

This is an honour song for Billy Jack
The only man who stepped up to raise me

The one good man who took my eyes
Made me see

Beyond the walls of welfare housing
Beyond the shame painting my mother's face

Step up, step up

He took his right foot and
He whopped them this side of their face

This is an honour song for Billy Jack
The only man who stepped up to protect me

The one decent man who took my terror
The scars from those who beat us

Watch his feet, watch his feet, boys
This is a snakebite ceremony

He is so above the law
He is going to whop you this side of your face

This is an honour song for Billy Jack
The only man who stepped up to show me

How to take on the town
How to duck the put-downs

How to stand up for your people
How to think in Indian

This an honour song for Billy Jack
The only man who stepped up to raise me

The one good man who took my hate
And made me think

Made me think
How to take my words, my words
Sing them down
Sing them down

Step up, step up, boy
Wop them this side of their face

This is an honour song for Billy Jack
The one good man who took my feet

And made me feel the earth
Made me plant my heels

So I was one
One with the vibrations of this land

Step up, step up, boy
This is an honour song for Billy Jack

The only man who stepped up to raise me
The one good man who took my hands

And made me see
Each finger is a weapon of creation

Each toe is a memory
Of the earth that holds you

Step up, step up, boy
I was seven in 1973

Dying in my skin
Holding up my mother's bones

I was seven and not five feet tall
Dying in my skin, the one tin soldier

This is an honour song for Billy jack
The only man who stepped up to raise me

Dangerous Sound

is this okay
this space of me to occupy

I apologize my skin
is not a good skin to be in

I'm not brown enough to testify
I apologize for my off-putting

beige hue, the discount colour
they sell at the fabric store

is this okay
this space of me to occupy

I apologize, me alone
because my aunty cannot say

what they did to her,
she cannot say

how they tied up her tongue,
how it went in order

something like this;
1 Hail Mary, 2 Hail Mary

3 Hail Mary, four.

I apologize her skin was not brown enough
to testify, it was not

torn enough to be noticed,
it was not viable enough

to be counted, to be reimbursed,
to be indemnified

because we are the colour
of exemption, a haze of beige

that is not permitted roads
on the maps of our own skin,
we are not permitted place names
to mark our losses

is this okay
this space of me to occupy

is this okay
I'm throwing my words like bibles,

I am choking on them like hymns
Is this okay

when I say
the Genesis of me is boiled tongues

and rapped knuckles
is this okay

this space of me to occupy
I'm clean like bleach

I'm in order like a picket fence,
I'm observant like a little lamb,

I'm upright as a crucifix
I am
her
voice,

the discounted colour
they sell at the fabric store

the beige hue that does not permit us
room on the shelves of history,

a haze of beige
that does not give us the words

to name our sorrow, to name
the names, and to name ourselves

accordingly

She Is Spitting a Mouthful of Stars

(nikâwi's Song)

She is spitting a mouthful of stars
She is laughing more than the men who beat her
She is ten horses breaking open the day
She is new to her bones
She is holy in the dust

She is spitting a mouthful of stars
She is singing louder than the men who raped her
She is waking beyond the Milky Way
She is new to her breath
She is sacred in this breathing

She is spitting a mouthful of stars
She is holding the light more than those who despised her
She is folding clouds in her movement
She is new to this sound
She is unbroken flesh

She is spitting a mouthful of stars
She is laughing more than those who shamed her
She is ten horses breaking open the day
She is new to these bones
She is holy in their dust

Her Testimony

For every dime I could not find my breath
mwâc kî-natotamwak   *No, they didn't listen*

For every dime I sat lonesome in dis place
mwâc kî-natotamwak

For every dime I drank for one of my boys
mwâc kî-natotamwak

For every dime I watched dah days go dragging on
mwâc kî-natotamwak

For every dime I made bread
mwâc kî-natotamwak

For every dime I fed ghosts
mwâc kî-natotamwak

For every dime I scrubbed my old man's clothes
mwâc kî-natotamwak

   Dese words might as well be dirty clothes
   hanging on dah clothesline

For every dime I drank away Ghristmas
mwâc kî-natotamwak

For every dime I prayed to God
mwâc kî-natotamwak

For every dime I spit blood
mwâc kî-natotamwak

For every dime I made new moccasins
mwâc kî-natotamwak

For every dime I dold a story
mwâc kî-natotamwak

For every dime I used dis guitar
mwâc kî-natotamwak

For every dime I sang a song
mwâc kî-natotamwak

  Dese words might as well be broken dishes
  stacked in dah cupboard

For every dime I watched a girl hit for bleeding
mwâc kî-natotamwak

For every dime I saw dah Brother's snake
mwâc kî-natotamwak

For every dime I ate dere leftovers
mwâc kî-natotamwak

For every dime I felt dah Sister's hands
mwâc kî-natotamwak

For every dime I cleaned dere sins
mwâc kî-natotamwak

For every dime my husband hit me
mwâc kînatotamwak

For every dime I could not find my breath
mwâc kî-natotamwak

  But dese words might as well be swept
  wit dah rugs, trown out

Me, dey say
I'm not an Indian woman

Only half, me

wit no countable wounds
mwâc kî-natotamwak

This Is Not a Manifesto

(Club Reprise)

box box ticketedy box   mark my words
hey-ya-hey-hey I'm not your quantum of pure blood

best blood   I'm the sinew of many nights mixing
the evidence of ancient bones grinding   red cells

binding to the white cliffs of my everyday face
mark my words   *hey-ya-hey-hey*

I'm not your country club turn-away   the caddy
for your prerequisite of skin   colour

tone it down, boy   I will not ever be brown enough
white enough to simply be   me

the half of a half of a half half half   the one little
two little three little   hatreds

I am made to wear   spit in my blue eye
but I see the world in Cree   *hey-ya-hey-hey*

I am part of this land   I am this land
split my guts and you'll see muskeg

I will not hang my head dappled with stars
I will not lay it down   no

so you can swing your axe of authenticity   so
you can keep the gene pool pure   once

I heard someone say we were mud breeds
as if the solution was to dry out the membership role

tally who's got white privilege   a white husband
in a white neighborhood

in a white town whitewashed by white industry
hey-ya-hey-hey   I dream in Cree

my chapan's halfbreed lingo   peyak   *one*
she didn't keep her head down

nîso   She didn't take the put downs   nisto   *two, three*
she didn't wear her teeth down

chewing and chewing and chewing
what they said she must swallow   no

she held proud her bones   *hey-ya-hey-hey*
never brown enough

never white enough   never good enough
to simply be a lifetime

member
this is not a manifesto   a declaration of red cells

a platform to defend my everyday face
spit in my blue eye

split my guts   I will never be brown enough
white enough to simply

be

Facebook Powwow

If I am not banging the drum
I am no one. No one, I am

No more than the Sunday spectator
Here to see the finery. I have no fancy feathers,

No Custer-killing steps.
Just this eagle bone whistle

Carved into the shape of my mouth
Screeching my neatly stitched life, the old regalia

That no longer fits, the new moccasins
To dance me into this arbour called my Being.

Once I was a flowing dancer.
I had all the right moves. I knew when to stop

On cue. I pulsed with the drum –
Hookah, I was a whirlwind of politics.

Show me your style, they said
And my style I did show –

Hookah, I was as bold as the Whip Man.
I swept the floor clean. I didn't spin for the monîyaw,   *whiteman*

I didn't sway for their swooning I didn't
Snap their pictures

To keep as testimony to then put in my book
Of what part of myself to later hate.

But now I am old without my beadwork and bustles.
Now I am between Traditional

And Chicken. I can barely screech this thing
Called my opinion. Still, I cannot shut up

On cue.
Once I was a flowing dancer, proud in my face.

Even then I was too white for the judges.
Show me your stripes, they said

And my stripes I did not show –
Hookah, I was as resistant as Louis,

As defiant as Gabe.
I will not split you my blood, I said –

Hookah, I was not sewn for this competition.
I was not made for your approval.

Once I was a flowing dancer.
Once I swirled with politics.

Unshakable were my feathers.
Militant were my feet.

But then I was made to spin with shame.
I was made to dance in black and white.

Then I sold my outfit.
Then I made a new one.

With this whistle carved from bone,
I announced my arrival.

Into the arena of myself I quietly came,
The drum of my blood

Ready for my own singing.

Since When

did I lose my step, in 2006
detectable by the check of the Census
I became the 389 thousand, 785th person
to name myself Metis

not the little m Metis
not the accent é Mé-tis
but the swinging   I'm jigging
through this line of invisibility

I'm Gabe stepping on their toes
reel in, reel out
real is what I'm dancing about
Metis

In 2006, check by check
I became the 389 thousand, 785th person
to choo-choo-choo my history
down Macdonald's railroad

to chug-chug-chug my halfbreed bones
not the little m bones,
not the accent é bones,
but the laying at Batoche bones,

the kill-me-if-you-can bones
because I'm jigging   swinging
through this line of invisibility
I'm Louis stepping on their toes

reel in, reel out
real is what I'm dancing about
Metis
In 2006, check by red blood check

I became my own thinning blood,
I became my own resistance
I became one of the 389 thousand, 785th persons
to brake the train, to cry *whoa*

hold up, hold up
how is it the seats on this train
tripled in capacity   how is it
we are scattered from coast to coast
when, in fact, we were denied a ticket
when, indeed, a drunkard's scheme
was to sweep the prairie clean
make us disappear   dis

appear   the little m metis
the accent é Mé-tis
a 91% growth in the size of our population
the choo-choo-choo of my inheritance

so I become the 389 thousand, 785th person
to name myself Metis
but I'm no little m Metis
I'm no accent é Mé-tis

but a stand-my-ground Metis
lay my bones at Batoche Metis
kill-me-if-you-can Metis
see me swinging   I'm jigging

past this line of invisibility
I'm Gabe stepping on their toes
reel in, reel out
real is what I'm dancing about

Metis

Despite

I persist. Anyway.
Still. Despite.
There is a sound left in my chest
And my ribs, not broken from all of this,
Take the shape of crows
Made from clay, made from water.
Here, I listen for songs.
pa-pum, pa-pum, pa-pum.
They persist. Anyway.
Still. Despite.

When I turn home, one day
My eyes hollow like the canyon
I will ride first to the east
Then to the west, to the south
And then onto home.
The crows, empty of songs, will be gone.
Again I will be clay.
Again I will be water drumming,
sha-shaa, sha-shaa, sha-shaa.
I will persist. Anyway.
Still. Despite.

Credible

If I stand here wooden
My hand above my brow, if

I keep my mouth shut, my eyes
Painted dull and stark, if

I stand here mute of words
Will I be credible, will I be seen?

If I stand here wooden
My feathers upright in their band, if

I keep my head in one place, my gaze
Fixed inconsolable and aimless, if

I stand here chiselled by two bigoted hands
Will I be credible, will I be seen?

If I stand here wooden
The scarlet robe across my chest, if

I let my hair fall
Black to my breast, if

I bend my knee, my legs
Two stumps keeping me in place, if

I keep my mouth shut, if
I hold this pose, this box of expectation

Of everything I should be
Will I be credible, will I be seen?

Notes & Acknowledgements

"She Is Spitting a Mouthful of Stars" has previously appeared in *Walrus Magazine*, summer 2016 issue.

"Her Testimony" has previously appeared in *The Fiddlehead*, summer 2016 issue.

The transcription of "sixty-one seconds of audio" in "Muskrat Woman" is of a conversation released by the RCMP between Amber Tuccaro and her presumed, unidentified abductor shortly after her disappearance and before her murder in August, 2010.

Hai-Hai to Lindsey "Eekwol" Knight for the line "I was born into this fair skin" in "Untitled."

About the Author

Gregory Scofield is Red River Metis of Cree, Scottish and European descent whose ancestry can be traced to the fur trade and to the Metis community of Kinesota, Manitoba. He has taught First Nations and Metis Literature and Creative Writing at Brandon University, Emily Carr University of Art + Design, and the Alberta College of Art + Design. He currently holds the position of Assistant Professor in English at Laurentian University where he teaches Creative Writing. Scofield won the Dorothy Livesay Poetry Prize in 1994 for his debut collection, *The Gathering: Stones for the Medicine Wheel*, and has since published seven further volumes of poetry as well as a memoir, *Thunder Through My Veins* (1999). Scofield has served as writer-in-residence at the University of Manitoba, University of Winnipeg and Memorial University.

Other Books by Gregory Scofield

The Gathering: Stones for the Medicine Wheel (poetry, 1993)
Native Canadiana: Songs from the Urban Rez (poetry, 1996)
Love Medicine and One Song (poetry, 1997)
I Knew Two Métis Women (poetry, 1999)
Thunder Through My Veins (memoir, 1999)
Singing Home the Bones (poetry, 2005)
kipocihkân: Poems New & Selected (poetry, 2009)
Louis: The Heretic Poems (poetry, 2011)
Wâpikwaniy: A Beginner's Guide to Metis Floral Beadwork (guide, 2011)
Maskisina: A Guide to Northern Style Metis Moccasins (guide, 2013)